DISCARD

WOMEN WHO WIN

Cynthia Cooper

Mia Hamm

Martina Hingis

Chamique Holdsclaw

Michelle Kwan

Lisa Leslie

Sheryl Swoopes

Venus & Serena Williams

CHELSEA HOUSE PUBLISHERS

WOMEN WHO WIN

SHERYL SWOOPES

Michael Burgan

Introduction by
HANNAH STORM

CHELSEA HOUSE PUBLISHERS
Philadelphia

Frontis: *A Texas state-wide champion and Olympic gold medalist, rising Comet Sheryl Swoopes is one of the Houston team's most valuable players, both on defense and offense.*

Produced by
21st Century Publishing and Communications, Inc.
New York, New York
http://www.21cpc.com

CHELSEA HOUSE PUBLISHERS

Editor in Chief: Stephen Reginald
Managing Editor: James D. Gallagher
Production Manager: Pamela Loos
Art Director: Sara Davis
Director of Photography: Judy L. Hasday
Senior Production Editor: J. Christopher Higgins
Publishing Coordinator: James McAvoy
Project Editor: Anne Hill

The Chelsea House World Wide Web address is
http://www.chelseahouse.com

First Printing

1 3 5 7 9 8 6 4 2

Library of Congress Cataloging-in-Publication Data

Burgan, Michael.
   Sheryl Swoopes / Michael Burgan; introduction by Hannah Storm.
   p. cm. – (Women who win)
   Includes bibliographical references and index.
   Summary: Presents a biography of the star player for the Houston Comets of the Women's National Basketball Association.
ISBN 0-7910-5795-X (hc) — ISBN 0-7910-6155-8 (pbk)
1. Swoopes, Sheryl—Juvenile literature. 2. Basketball players—United States—Biography—Juvenile literature. 3. Women basketball players—United States—Biography—Juvenile literature. [1. Swoopes, Sheryl. 2. Basketball players. 3. Women—Biography. 4. Afro-Americans—Biography.] I. Title. II. Series.

GV884.S88 B89 2000
796.323'092—dc21
[B]   00—022583
                                                              CIP
                                                               AC

CONTENTS

INTRODUCTION   6

CHAPTER 1
WHAT A WEEK!   9

CHAPTER 2
BECOMING THE BEST   17

CHAPTER 3
ROAD TO A CHAMPIONSHIP   23

CHAPTER 4
GOLDEN MOMENTS   31

CHAPTER 5
GO FOR THE PROS   39

CHAPTER 6
PART OF THE TEAM   47

CHAPTER 7
THREE-PEAT   55

STATISTICS   61
CHRONOLOGY   62
FURTHER READING   62
INDEX   64

WOMEN WHO WIN

Hannah Storm
NBC Studio Host

You go girl! Women's sports are the hottest thing going right now, with the 1900s ending in a big way. When the U.S. team won the 1999 Women's World Cup, it captured the imagination of all sports fans and served as a great inspiration for young girls everywhere to follow their dreams.

That was just the exclamation point on an explosive decade for women's sports—capped off by the Olympic gold medals for the U.S. women in hockey, softball, and basketball. All the excitement created by the U.S. national basketball team helped to launch the Women's National Basketball Association (WNBA), which began play in 1997. The fans embraced the concept, and for the first time, a successful and stable women's professional basketball league was formed.

I was the first ever play-by-play announcer for the WNBA—a big personal challenge. Broadcasting, just like sports, had some areas with limited opportunities for women. There have traditionally not been many play-by-play opportunities for women in sports television, so I had no experience. To tell you the truth, the challenge I faced was a little scary! Sometimes we are all afraid that we might not be up to a certain task. It is not easy to take risks, but unless we push ourselves we will stagnate and not grow.

Here's what happened to me. I had always wanted to do play-by-play earlier in my career, but I had never gotten the opportunity. Not that I was unhappy—I had been given studio hosting assignments that were unprecedented for a woman and my reputation was well established in the business. I was comfortable in my role . . . plus I had just had my first baby. The last thing I needed to do was suddenly tackle a new skill on national television and risk being criticized (not to mention, very stressed out!). Although I had always wanted to do play-by-play, I turned down the assignment twice, before reluctantly agreeing to give it a try. During my hosting stint of the NBA finals that year, I traveled back and forth to WNBA preseason games to practice play-by-play. I was on 11 flights in 14 days to seven different cities! My head was spinning and it was no surprise that I got sick. On the day of the first broadcast, I had to have shots just so I could go on the air without throwing up. I felt terrible and nervous, but

I survived my first game. I wasn't very good but gradually, week by week, I got better. By the end of the season, the TV reviews of my work were much better—*USA Today* called me "most improved."

During that 1997 season, I witnessed a lot of exciting basketball moments, from the first historic game to the first championship, won by the Houston Comets. The challenge of doing play-by-play was really exciting and I loved interviewing the women athletes and seeing the fans' enthusiasm. Over one million fans came to the games; my favorite sight was seeing young boys wearing the jerseys of female players—pretty cool. And to think I almost missed out on all of that. It reinforced the importance of taking chances and not being afraid of challenges or criticism. When we have an opportunity to follow our dreams, we need to go for it!

Thankfully, there are now more opportunities than ever for women in sports (and other areas, like broadcasting). We thank women, like those in this series, who have persevered despite lack of opportunities—women who have refused to see their limitations. Remember, women's sports has been around a long time. Way back in 396 B.C. Kyniska, a Spartan princess, won an Olympic chariot race. Of course, women weren't allowed to compete, so she was not allowed to collect her prize in person. At the 1996 Olympic games in Atlanta, Georgia, over 35,600 women competed, almost a third more than in the previous Summer Games. More than 20 new women's events have been added for the Sydney, Australia, Olympics in 2000. Women's collegiate sports continues to grow, spurred by the 1972 landmark legislation Title IX, which states that "no person in the United States shall, on the basis of sex, be excluded from participation in, be denied the benefits of, or be subjected to discrimination under any educational program or activity receiving federal financial assistance." This has set the stage for many more scholarships and opportunities for women, and now we have professional leagues as well. No longer do the most talented basketball players in the country have to go to Europe or Asia to earn a living.

The women in this series did not have as many opportunities as you have today. But they were persistent through all obstacles, both on the court and off. I can tell you that Cynthia Cooper is the strongest woman I know. What is it that makes Cynthia and the rest of the women included in this series so special? They are not afraid to share their struggles and their stories with us. Their willingness to show us their emotions, open their hearts, bare their souls, and let us into their lives is what, in my mind, separates them from their male counterparts. So accept this gift of their remarkable stories and be inspired. Because *you*, too, have what it takes to follow your dreams.

1

WHAT A WEEK!

F or the Houston Comets, the 1999 basketball season started just as it had two years before, when they won the championship. The team was the very first champion in a new women's basketball league, the Women's National Basketball Association (WNBA). In 1998, the players won their second championship, and halfway through the third season, the Comets were once again the best team in the WNBA.

Women had only briefly played professional basketball in the 1970s, but times have changed since then. Women's basketball has grown tremendously. Now thousands of fans come to the games, while millions more watch on TV. Girls who play basketball can dream about becoming pros, just as boys do. Young female players also have their own heroes, one of whom plays for the Houston Comets. Her name is Sheryl Swoopes.

Sheryl is one of the superstars of women's basketball. In 1993, she led her college team to a national championship. At the 1996 Summer Olympics, she helped the U.S. team win the gold medal in women's basketball. When the

Eluding her guard, Sheryl goes for a shot during a championship game with the Detroit Shock. No one could deny Sheryl her week of triumph in the 1999 season, when she made history by becoming the first WNBA player to record a triple-double.

WNBA formed in 1997, she was already a famous basketball star.

At 6', Sheryl is not one of the tallest players in the WNBA. She is not the strongest either. She may be the hardest worker, however, and she is certainly one of the most talented women ever to play the game of basketball. Sheryl's college coach said of her, "She'll be a legend in women's basketball." The Comets' coach, Van Chancellor, simply describes Sheryl as "a big-time player."

Sheryl plays forward, which means her main job is to score points. She uses her blazing quickness to get around defenders and drive for the basket. Away from the hoop, she has an accurate jump shot, making her difficult to guard. Sheryl also makes assists—passing the ball to help her teammates score. When the opponents have the ball and Sheryl is on defense, she often steals the ball from them and blocks their shot attempts. At either end of the court, she fights for rebounds. Said her teammate Tina Thompson, "She does it all for us."

On July 27, 1999, Sheryl showed all her talents in one game. She and her teammates were playing the Detroit Shock. The Shock featured guard Sandy Brondello, who had just played in the WNBA All-Star game. Only the league's best players were chosen for that match. Still, the Comets were clearly the better team, which included three All-Stars of their own: Cynthia Cooper, Tina Thompson, and Sheryl. So far in the 1999 season, the Comets had lost only four of their first 20 games. No one expected the two-time–champion Comets to lose this game, but no one knew what else would happen that night, either.

Sheryl didn't score her first points for almost seven minutes until she was fouled and given two free throws—shots made with no defenders around her. She sank them both and gave Houston a 10-7 lead. Even without scoring much, Sheryl was playing well. She had already grabbed a few rebounds and made a few assists. She then added another basket and a steal. At halftime, the Comets were ahead 37-17.

In the second half, Sheryl continued to play well all over the court, being particularly fierce on the boards. With just a few minutes left in the game, she had 15 rebounds, her most ever since becoming a pro. She had also scored 14 points. Coach Van Chancellor went over to Sheryl and told her, "I'm giving you one minute."

Confused by the direction, she did not understand exactly what Chancellor was referring to. "One minute for what?" she asked. She didn't know that she was about to make history.

With four minutes and 15 seconds to play, Sheryl dished off the ball to her teammate Amaya Valdemoro, who then pushed hard to the basket and scored. With that pass to Valdemoro, Sheryl had made her 10th assist of the game, another career high as a pro. Along with her totals for points and rebounds, Sheryl had recorded a triple-double—double figures in three different categories: scoring, rebounding, and assists. Triple-doubles are rare in basketball, and only a player with amazing abilities can do it. Sheryl had become the first WNBA player to achieve that feat.

Coach Chancellor called a short time-out. As Sheryl walked off the court, the Houston fans gave her an standing ovation. After the

With a Phoenix Mercury player trying to run her down, Sheryl scores a basket. Her scoring in this game gave the Comets the victory and earned Sheryl the honor of being named Player of the Week.

game, when talking to reporters, she commented, "I wasn't concentrating on points or rebounds or anything tonight. I just went out there and played. I feel like if I went out and did the same things I've been doing all night, eventually it was going to come." Sheryl referred to getting the triple-double as "a lot of fun and definitely a great honor."

Jen Rizzotti, another Comets player who was on the floor when Sheryl made history, summed up the feelings of many players and fans, saying: "I'm just so happy for Sheryl and I'm a little surprised that the triple-double hasn't come sooner than this. She's been so close before that it was just a matter of time."

Two days later, Sheryl and the Comets headed to Cleveland, Ohio. The Cleveland Rockers had been one of the best teams in the WNBA in 1998, but this season they were struggling. Still, the Rockers played well in this game with the Comets. At the beginning of the match, Houston played poorly, missing seven of their first eight shots. Only Sheryl was able to find the basket. She scored 13 of her team's points in the first half, and at half-time the Comets trailed 34-26.

In the second half, the Comets fell behind by 13 points. Then, they began to improve their defense, stealing their passes and putting intense pressure on the Rockers as soon as any of their players touched the ball. On offense, Houston started scoring. With about eight minutes to go, Sheryl passed to Cynthia Cooper on a fast break. Racing down the court, Cooper scored a layup. The Comets led for the first time in this game. A few minutes later, Swoopes stole the ball again. Now it was her turn to score on the fast break. Houston was in the lead 65-58.

The Rockers fought back and were down by only four points with 11 seconds to go when Sheryl was fouled. She sank two free throws, adding to the Comets' lead. Houston won 71-65. Sheryl finished with 28 points, the most of any player on either team.

The Comets played their last game of the regular season in July at home. Their opponent was the Phoenix Mercury, a team Houston had beaten in the 1998 championship series. In this game, however, Phoenix jumped out to a quick lead. By the end of the first half, the Comets came back and were in control.

The Mercury refused to quit. With about a minute to play, they were only down by seven points, and it was possible that they still could win. With Houston holding the ball, Sheryl took a pass and forced her way to the basket. A score—and a foul! She made the free throw and Houston led 71-60. The Comets held on to win 77-70. "I thought that [the three-point play] was the turning point in the game," Sheryl told reporters afterward.

Finishing this game with 23 points, once again, Sheryl was the high scorer for both teams. She had just ended one of her best weeks as a pro. For the three games played that week, she averaged 21.7 points. She also had an average of 9.3 rebounds, 5.3 assists, and 2.33 steals. The WNBA honored Sheryl for her triple-double and her all-around great play by naming her the Player of the Week.

With the season more than half over, Sheryl Swoopes was among the league's leaders in almost every category. The Comets also had a good chance to win their third championship in a row.

Despite all her success, however, Sheryl knows that life is not always easy. She has known what it is like to be disappointed. In the past, she had lost big games, and she had faced personal losses as well. Still, Sheryl Swoopes always keeps a positive attitude. "It's my experience," she wrote in her book *Bounce Back*, "that no matter how far life pushes you down, no matter how much you hurt, you can always bounce back."

2

BECOMING
THE BEST

S heryl learned her basketball skills while growing up in
Brownfield, Texas, where she was born on March 25,
1971. Brownfield is a small farming town in northwest
Texas. The nearest big city is Lubbock, about 40 miles
away. Sheryl lived with her mother, Louise Swoopes, and
her brothers, James and Earl. (Another brother, Brandon,
came along later.) Sheryl's father had left the family before
she was born, and Louise sometimes worked three jobs to
keep her children clothed and fed.

Sheryl knew that her family was poor. When friends
asked her to go shopping, all she could do was look. "I didn't
have the money to buy anything," she later recalled. The
Swoopes had deep religious beliefs and a strong sense of
family, however, and Sheryl never stopped dreaming of
what she could become.

Her first dream was to be a cheerleader. She and her
cousin often dressed up as cheerleaders and rooted for
Sheryl's brothers when they played basketball. In sixth
grade, Sheryl joined the pep squad, but she never became
a real cheerleader. When she was old enough to join the

---

*From her childhood, Sheryl wanted to be a professional basket-
ball player. Becoming the best she could be meant years of work
and practice. Through high school and college and on to the WNBA,
Sheryl never wavered in her determination to reach her goal.*

team, her family didn't have enough money to buy the uniform and shoes. By this time, however, Sheryl had discovered basketball.

When her brothers went out to play basketball, little sister Sheryl was never far behind. The Swoopes boys shot the ball at the rim from an old bicycle wheel, which was nailed to a piece of plywood. At the beginning, Sheryl begged Earl and James to let her play.

"Basketball is for boys," they said. "You can't play." A stubborn seven-year-old, Sheryl kept pleading. Finally, her brothers gave in, but they were determined not to go easy on her. The boys played keep-away, tossing the ball to each other so Sheryl couldn't get it. When she did touch the ball, she was sure to get a push or a shove. "They'd throw me the ball so hard it'd knock me in the head." she recalled. "I'd run inside crying and tell Mom." Sheryl refused to quit, however. "Every time they pushed me down . . . I'd wipe dry my tears and go back out to play."

Years later, James told a reporter the reason he and Earl were so hard on Sheryl: "We were just trying to toughen her up." It must have worked. She learned from her brothers how to dribble and shoot, playing in a game called 21—the first person to score 21 points wins. During her first years as a basketball novice, Sheryl couldn't beat James and Earl, but that day would soon come.

Shortly after her first games with her brothers, Sheryl joined a basketball team in a league called Little Dribblers. She had a goal to reach on the court—someday she would win an Olympic gold medal in basketball.

As a Little Dribbler, Sheryl was already tall for her age, and she picked up the nickname "Legs." In her third year with the Little Dribblers, she helped her team reach the national champion-ships. Although the final game was close, Sheryl and her teammates lost by a few points. "I felt I let the team down," Sheryl wrote in her book, "and it took awhile for me to bounce back."

In junior high school, Sheryl played volleyball and basketball and dreamed of playing for the high school varsity team. Her chance came in her freshman year when, after one basketball game with the junior varsity team, Sheryl was invited to join the high school varsity team. Once again, she improved her skills by playing with boys, and once again, she went through some rough times on the court.

On summer nights, Sheryl headed to the gym, always hoping the boys would need an extra player. Otherwise, all she could do was watch. When the boys did let Sheryl play, they mostly ignored her. She later remembered, "The only time I got to shoot was if I got the rebound and dribbled the length of the court myself." She could feel anger building inside her as the boys made fun of her skills. "But I swallowed my pride to play," Sheryl said, "because I knew it would make me a stronger player."

Sheryl was right about becoming stronger. In 1987, as a sophomore, she was named to the All-State team. The honor recognized her talents as one of the best high school basketball players in Texas. In her junior year, she was the best player on the Cubs—the Brownfield High School girls' team. Sheryl led the Cubs to a 29-8 record and a shot at the state championship.

The Cubs entered the title game as the under-dog—no one expected the team to win. Their opponent was the Hardin–Jefferson High School team, which had not lost all season. At half-time, the Cubs trailed 25-19. In the second half,

At Brownfield High School, Sheryl helped lead her team, the Cubs, to a state championship by playing superb offense and defense. Sheryl was on her way to achieving her goal of becoming a basketball pro.

however, Sheryl began to take charge. As one of the tallest players on the team, her strength was playing inside—near the basket, and she began sinking shots. With six minutes to go, the Cubs took the lead and held on for a 49-40 victory. Brownfield had won its first state championship, and Sheryl had led the Cubs with 26 points and 18 rebounds. To cap off this great season, she was once again named to the All-State team.

After Brownfield won the championship in 1988, Sheryl and her teammates expected yet another great year. Instead, the next season included some disappointments. The Cubs did reach the state tournament, but this time Brownfield was beaten early. In the losing game, Sheryl claimed she played poorly: "Once again I had a sick feeling inside that I let everyone down—my teammates, coaches, school, and town." Nevertheless, Sheryl played well and was named All-State a third time. Her play was also drawing the attention of basketball experts from around the country, and she was named to three All-American high school teams—teams that honor the best players in the country.

No one could criticize Sheryl's playing at Brownfield. During her four years there, she averaged 26 points and 14 rebounds with five assists and five steals per game. On both offense and defense, she was a star.

It was time to move on to college, and many schools across the country wanted Sheryl to play on their women's basketball teams. She chose to stay in Texas and to study and play at the University of Texas in Austin, about 400 miles from Brownfield.

Sports teams at the University of Texas are called the Longhorns. The Lady Longhorns basketball team had won the National Collegiate Athletic Association (NCAA) championship in 1986. (The NCAA is in charge of sports for major U.S. colleges and universities.) The team had gone undefeated in the 1986 season, and Texas fans hoped Sheryl would lead the Lady Longhorns to another NCAA championship.

After just a few days at the university, however, Sheryl sensed something was wrong. The school "felt too big and too far from home," she later wrote. She missed her family and her high school sweetheart, Eric Jackson. Her mother remembered that Sheryl didn't feel right about going to the University of Texas even before she left for school. Louise Swoopes recalled, "I think she started on a Monday, and every day she called and said, 'Mom, I want to come home.' . . . On Friday she was home."

Some of Sheryl's friends wondered why she left the university, saying she would never have another chance to play for a powerful team and win the NCAA championship. Sheryl, however, still believed she could reach her goal of having a successful college basketball career. It would just take a little more time and work.

3

ROAD TO A CHAMPIONSHIP

Back home in Brownfield, Sheryl made a phone call. She talked to Lyndon Hardin, the women's basketball coach at South Plains College, a two-year college (also called a junior college). When she told Coach Hardin she wanted to play for his Lady Texans team, he thought she was joking. Why would a great player like Sheryl want to play for his school?

For one thing, South Plains is in Levelland, just 30 miles from Brownfield. For another, Sheryl could play right away at South Plains since it was a junior college. Under the NCAA's rules, she would have had to sit out a year if she went to another four-year college. Once he got over his disbelief, Hardin welcomed Sheryl to the team.

Sheryl noted one difference between high school and college basketball. More of the college players were as tall as she was, if not taller. By now, Sheryl was close to 6' and was used to towering over her opponents and playing close to the basket. At South Plains, she had to improve her outside shot so that her offensive game would be more complete.

At Texas Tech, Sheryl celebrates a victory over Ohio State by cutting down the net. As one of Texas Tech's Lady Raiders, Sheryl kept setting scoring records and winning honors. She was on her way to being recognized nationally as a top player in women's college basketball.

In her first season at South Plains, Sheryl led the Lady Texans to a 27-9 record and the Western Junior College Conference championship. She set a school scoring record on November 30, 1989, when she poured in 45 points against Clarendon College. A few weeks later, she put her name in the school record books again, grabbing 22 rebounds in a game against Phoenix College.

Sheryl finished the 1989–90 season with a scoring average of 25.6, which led the league and placed her in the top 10 nationally. Her other averages that season were just as impressive: 11.5 rebounds, 4.7 steals, and 1.94 blocked shots per game. The National Junior College Athletic Association (NJCAA) named Sheryl to its All-American team, as did Kodak, a company that also honors the best players in women's college basketball.

The following season was another strong one for Sheryl and the Lady Texans. The team went 25-4, and Sheryl was once again named an NJCAA and Kodak All-American. She finished with just under 25 points and 11.9 rebounds per game. In 1991, the Women's Basketball Coaches' Association named Sheryl the Junior College Player of the Year.

South Plains coach Lyndon Hardin certainly agreed with that honor. After coaching and watching his amazing star player for two seasons, Hardin commented, "I've never been around anyone that's as talented and has the basketball savvy that she has, and I don't know if I ever will again."

It was time for Sheryl to move on, however. She left South Plains and reentered a four-year college. This time she chose Texas Tech in Lubbock, Texas, and played for the women's basketball team as a Lady Raider. Sheryl was ready to show what she had learned since her short stay at the University of Texas.

Unlike the University of Texas, Texas Tech was not a major force in women's college basketball at that time. Under coach Marsha Sharp, however, the Lady Raiders were improving and Sheryl's joining the team certainly added great force. During the 1991–92 season, Sheryl's first season with the team, Texas Tech finished first in the Southwest Conference (SWC). The team then went on to win its first SWC tournament championship. In the NCAA tournament, the Lady Raiders played the best college teams in the country. They won their first games but eventually lost to Stanford University.

For Sheryl, the year was another success. She scored 21.6 points per game and added 8.9 rebounds. She had three triple-doubles, the first ever by a Lady Raider. She was also named the SWC Player of the Year and once again earned All-American honors.

In the spring of 1992, she had a chance to make one of her lifelong dreams come true: to play basketball for the U.S. women's team in the Olympics. Sheryl went to the tryouts, but partway through one practice, she twisted her ankle. The sprain was bad enough to keep her from playing in the tryouts, and she would not be going to the Olympics. Eventually, the U.S. women's basketball team finished a disappointing third in the 1992 Olympic Games.

Back in Lubbock for her spring courses, Sheryl was crushed by her bad luck. "At that moment," she later wrote in her book, "I was ready to give up basketball and find another career and forget about ever playing again." Then, a chance meeting changed her mind.

While walking through a local mall, a young girl approached Sheryl and told her that every night she and her mother prayed for her. Before she walked away, the little girl added, "I don't want you to give up."

This brief conversation stunned Sheryl. "I stood frozen for several minutes and felt chills all over my body. Her simple message jolted me back to thinking positive." When the Texas Tech Lady Raiders returned to the court in the fall, Sheryl was ready to play the best basketball of her life.

The Lady Raiders started the 1992–93 season with 12 wins in the first 15 games and finished the season with the best record in the SWC. In the championship game of the league tournament, Texas Tech faced its rival from across the state, the University of Texas.

For Sheryl, this championship game was extra special. She was determined to show the University of Texas how good she had become since leaving that school. She had already scored 37 points against the Lady Longhorns at their last meeting during the regular season. This game meant much more, however.

The SWC championship game was played at the Dallas Reunion Arena, home of the Dallas Mavericks of the National Basketball Association (NBA)—the men's professional basketball league. Sheryl put on her own show as brilliantly as any NBA player, scoring 53 points. Her total was the highest ever scored in the arena, beating the old scoring record held by NBA superstars Larry Bird and Bernard King. Thanks to Sheryl's hot hand, Texas Tech won the championship 78-71.

After the victory, the Lady Raiders once again headed to the NCAA tournament. This year, though, was different from 1992; the Raiders

Although the U.S. women's team came in third in the 1992 Olympics, its players made a strong showing. Here, USA's Suzie McConnell snatches the ball from a Cuban player, an offensive move that helped the U.S. team defeat Cuba 88-74.

had the best women's player in America, and she was at the top of her game. Texas Tech cruised through its first four games to reach the semifinals in Atlanta. When she wasn't practicing, Sheryl was receiving honors for her fantastic season. When her mom drove to Atlanta to watch her daughter play, it was the first time Louise Swoopes had ever left Texas. Sheryl made the trip worthwhile.

In the semifinal game, Texas Tech faced the Commodores of Tennessee's Vanderbilt University. Sheryl had averaged 32.5 points per game so far in the tournament. She stayed close to that record in the game against the

Commodores, finishing with 31 points and 11 rebounds. Texas Tech won 60-46.

Next up was Ohio State and the championship game. Before the finals, Sheryl was nervous as she thought back to other big games in the past. Sometimes she felt that she had let her teammates down. This time, though, she knew things would be different.

Early in the game, Sheryl took her first shot—and missed. But the next one went in. And the next. Then two more. After that first miss, she made 10 shots in a row. "At a point in the game," Sheryl commented later, "I felt I wanted to personally take control." The 16,000 fans packed into the arena sensed they were seeing a special performance. Cries of "Swoopes, Swoopes!" filled the air. At halftime, Sheryl had 23 points and Texas Tech led by 9.

Sheryl continued her great play in the second half. "When I'm shooting well," she explained, "it's like the basket is as big as [a] table. I can't seem to miss." But Ohio State managed to stay close. With about a minute left, the Lady Raiders led by just four points. Suddenly Sheryl grabbed the ball and drove to the basket. Facing three defenders who stood in her way, she split the first two and darted between them. Then, with a lightning-fast change of direction, Sheryl cut around the third defender to get to the basket and score. She also drew a foul on the play and sank her free throw. Texas Tech was up by seven and held on to win 84-82.

Sheryl didn't realize that she had set another record. With 47 points, she had scored the most points ever in an NCAA championship game—men's or women's. Ohio State's coach, Nancy Darsch, told reporters, "You don't really appreciate Sheryl Swoopes until you have to stop her. We had made some plans to contain her. . . . But she answered everything we tried." Sheryl, however, was not so impressed with her performance. In her book she noted, "I never thought about individual statistics during the game. All I cared about was winning."

Along with the national championship, Sheryl once again won many honors. She was an All-American and the National Player of the Year and was also named the Female Athlete of 1993. Many basketball fans compared her to Michael Jordan—"Air Jordan," the greatest basketball player of the era. Jordan was also Sheryl's basketball idol. When the amazing season was over, Texas Tech coach Marsha Sharp said, "[t]here are no words to explain how great a player Sheryl Swoopes is."

4

GOLDEN MOMENTS

Winning the NCAA championship turned the Lady Raiders into basketball heroes. When the team returned to Lubbock, thousands of fans cheered them at the airport. A celebration on campus drew 35,000 people to the Texas Tech football stadium. President Bill Clinton also invited the team to the White House.

Sheryl, of course, was the biggest hero of all. Wherever she went, people crowded around her and asked for her autograph. She once spent hours signing and talking with her fans. "It's been wild and crazy," Sheryl told reporters. The only way to avoid the attention, Sheryl said, was to stay home.

In April 1993, a team in the United States Basketball League (USBL) asked Sheryl to play for them. Although the USBL was a men's professional league, it was not at the same level as the NBA. Sheryl was only the third woman ever selected to play in the league, but she rejected the offer. "It was a great honor," she said, "but I wouldn't have gotten to play." And playing basketball was the most important

Her dream of a U.S. Olympic win fulfilled, Sheryl (far right) and her teammates raise their arms in celebration of their gold medal at the 1996 Atlanta games. For Sheryl, the Olympics was the culmination of three years of a hectic schedule playing international tournaments with the U.S. Women's National Team.

thing in Sheryl's life. She still had her childhood goal: to reach the Olympics.

At the time, the United States had no professional basketball league for women, and Sheryl left Texas in August to play in Italy. Playing in Europe was an opportunity for many talented U.S. women to make money and keep their skills sharp. Sheryl wanted to make sure she was at her best when she tried out for the U.S. Olympic team.

Her experiences in Italy were not happy, however. On the court, she played with her usual talent. In 10 games, she averaged 23 points. But off the court, she had problems with the team's owner. Her boyfriend, Eric Jackson, who had gone to Italy with Sheryl, described what happened: "The owner of the team would tell us to meet him at the bank on Thursday so he could pay her. Then he wouldn't show up." Sheryl, who was very unhappy with the situation, said, "If I'm going to play basketball and not get paid, I'm going to do it in some gym in Texas."

In October, Sheryl returned to Lubbock. She took courses at Texas Tech and worked as a radio announcer during the Lady Raiders' basketball games. During her free time, she often went to the gym and practiced her moves. The workouts, she wrote, were "lonely and boring," but they also reminded her that "to get anywhere you have to be willing to do something extra every day to improve."

Making history one more time helped ease some of Sheryl's boredom. In February 1994, she appeared in an ad promoting Nike sneakers— the first female athlete to be featured in an advertisement for the shoe company. In the ad, Sheryl talked about her workouts, playing with

Endorsing products not only gave Sheryl some extra money but helped young people see her as a role model for women's athletics. Here, with WNBA stars Lisa Leslie (center) and Nikki McCray (right), Sheryl shows off a milk mustache for one of the popular ads.

her brothers in the early years, and becoming "a black female role model for younger kids."

That summer, Sheryl finally had a chance to compete in a real game. She made the U.S. National Team, which was traveling to Australia for the World Championships. In the second game, Sheryl had her best performance, scoring 27 points, and her team won 86-77. When the tournament was over, the U.S. team had finished third. Sheryl's averages were lower than those of her best years at Texas Tech. She played just 17 minutes per game and scored an average of 9.1 points. "My game was kind of rusty," she said after the tournament. Still, she called her trip a good experience. "I got a little playing time and got some of that international experience behind me."

International experience would be important for Sheryl when she once again tried out for the U.S. women's Olympic basketball team. International basketball games, men's and women's, are much rougher than college basketball. "Its kind of blood and guts," Sheryl explained. "Going to the hole [the basket], I have to expect to get fouled and fouled hard. I can't let it distract or change my game."

After the World Championships in Australia, Sheryl played in another international tournament, the Goodwill Games, helping the U.S. team win the gold medal. Then, once again, Sheryl returned to the gym in Lubbock to practice, playing against men who challenged her to show how good she was.

Sheryl also had a chance to play against her idol, Michael Jordan. The superstar ran a basketball camp for young players, and he asked Sheryl to work for him. One day, she and Michael played a game of one-on-one (no other players are on the court), and Sheryl scored the first three points. Michael soon took over, however. "Just don't dunk on me," Sheryl warned him. Replying that he couldn't disappoint his fans, he launched one of his monstrous dunks. Without thinking, Sheryl wrapped her arms around Michael and pulled him down to earth. "Oh my gosh," she thought, "I just fouled Michael Jordan!" The foul didn't stop him though, and he went on to win the game 7-5. For Sheryl it was just a thrill to play.

Nineteen ninety-five was an important year for Sheryl. In June, she married Eric Jackson. Later in the year, Nike introduced a sneaker named for Sheryl—"Air Swoopes," the first sneaker ever named for a woman. The most important event of the year for Sheryl, however, was going to the tryouts for the U.S. Olympic team, which came right before her and Eric's wedding.

Sheryl was one of the top 27 women players competing for just 12 spots on the team. She described the tryouts as "intense and nerve-wracking," but when they ended, Sheryl was on the team. She would play in the 1996 Summer Olympics in Atlanta, Georgia.

Before reaching the games, Sheryl and her teammates had plenty of work to do. They practiced for three months and then set off to play a 52-game schedule, traveling across the United States and to four continents. When the tour was over, the team had logged 102,000 miles. Sheryl found the trip exhausting. "I'd wake up and not remember what city I was visiting," she later recalled. Some days, when she felt she couldn't go on, she remembered why she had worked so hard—to play in the Olympics. She couldn't quit without reaching her dream.

The U.S. Women's National Team won all 52 games during its long tour. Finally, in July 1996, the Olympic games began. In the first game, the USA played Cuba and won 101-84 with Sheryl scoring 12 points. As the Americans cruised through their next six games, Sheryl had her best performance against Australia, scoring 17 in a 96-79 win. In their last game, the American players faced the Brazilian team for the gold medal.

Basketball superstar Michael "Air" Jordan is one of Sheryl's most enthusiastic fans. He has been such a long-time hero to Sheryl that she named her son, Jordan, after him.

In the semifinals of the Olympic Games, Australia's guard Roben Maher tries desperately to keep Sheryl from getting off a shot. Sheryl emerged from this game with her best performance, scoring 17 points against Australia.

Brazil was a tough, high-scoring team. Like the United States, Brazil had not lost a game during the Olympics. Sheryl knew firsthand about the Brazilians from the 1994 World Championships, when she and her teammates had lost to Brazil in the semifinals.

This time, only Brazil stood in the way of the United States winning the gold medal. The game was especially important for the American players because they were in front of a home crowd. Also, the U.S. team had won the Olympic gold medals in 1984 and 1988 and then finished third in 1992, winning the bronze medal. Sheryl and the current team wanted to show that the United States was once again the best in women's basketball.

Sheryl was given a tough job. Coach Tara VanDerveer assigned her to guard the best scorer on the Brazilian team, and Sheryl was eager to stop her opponent. She was probably too eager. She committed two quick fouls and was called to the bench, where the coach calmed her down and advised her to play smart. Sheryl recalled later, "I went back on the court and made the most of my second chance."

From then on, Sheryl and her teammates played tight defense and also shot well from inside. The game ended with the United States on top 111-87. As the Americans celebrated, a man approached Sheryl and told her that he had just watched great basketball. "He didn't say great women's basketball," Sheryl noted afterward. "He said great basketball. And that's exactly what we wanted to show the world—that we can play."

Sheryl scored 16 points in that final game and also had three rebounds and five assists. For the tournament, she averaged 13 points per game, third-best on the team, was second in steals with 12, and tied for first in blocks with five. Her individual play wasn't what counted, however. It was the thrill of knowing she had made her dream come true. As they received their gold medals, the American players cried tears of pride and joy. That night, Sheryl went to sleep with her medal safely tucked under her pillow.

GO FOR
THE PROS

During the 1996 Summer Olympic Games, millions of
Americans watched on TV as Sheryl Swoopes and the
U.S. women's basketball team won the gold medal. For
many people, it was probably the first time they had seen
a women's game, and basketball fans now realized that
women played hard and well. Sheryl and her teammates
had given a great boost to the sport.

Earlier in 1996, the American Basketball League (ABL),
a new women's professional league, had been formed and
announced it would play its first games in the fall. A year
later, another pro league for woman was formed, the
Women's National Basketball Association, which was
sponsored by the NBA. Prior to the organization of the
ABL and the WNBA, women had no chance to play professional basketball in the United States. Now they had two
choices.

Many of the players on the Olympic team had already
decided to play in the ABL even before the Olympics. At
first, Sheryl wasn't sure which league she should choose.
She told a reporter, "I'm just happy I've got some options,

*In the pros at last, Sheryl (right) and Olympic teammate Rebecca
Lobo have reason to smile as they proudly show off the jerseys
they prepared to wear for the first season of WNBA play.*

that I don't have to play in Europe." Finally, after winning the gold medal, she made her decision: she would play in the WNBA.

One of the first three players to sign a contract with the WNBA, Sheryl was immediately considered a top star in the new league. The two others were her Olympic teammates Rebecca Lobo and Lisa Leslie. Thrilled to be in the WNBA, Sheryl explained how the league "is providing an important opportunity for girls to have female role models and will demonstrate to the world what a great sport women's basketball is."

The WNBA assigned its players to teams located close to their former colleges, so Sheryl would be going back to Texas to play for the Houston Comets. Before she ever put on a Comets uniform, however, Sheryl's life took a different turn. Just after joining the WNBA, she announced that she was going to have a baby. "It wasn't planned," she told reporters, "but I'm ready. This is part of my life I had always looked forward to." Since the baby was due in late June—the same time the WNBA would play its first game—Sheryl would have to delay her start as a professional.

The WNBA season was set for 30 games, and fans wondered if Sheryl would be able to play at all that year. Even though she was eager to play pro games, her baby was more important to her at this point in her life. "I am going to take it one day at time," Sheryl said. "I'm not going to rush back. If it happens this season, fine, and if it doesn't, I know I will just have to wait until next summer."

While she was pregnant, Sheryl tried to stay in shape, exercising and practicing for as long as she could. As time went on, however, Sheryl found it more and more difficult to play the way she used to. "The hardest thing for me is not being able to just get up and go," Sheryl explained. "Before, I could go out, play basketball all day and never get tired."

In the spring of 1997, when Michael Jordan visited Sheryl and Eric, the couple asked him a favor. If the baby was a boy, could they name him after the superstar? Michael put his hands on Sheryl's stomach, paused, and then said it was okay—as long as the baby had a good jump shot. Kidding along with her hero, Sheryl replied,"Shoot, he's going to be better than you ever were."

A few months later, on June 25, Sheryl gave birth to her son, Jordan Eric. Speaking to a reporter about her excitement at being a mother, Sheryl said, "It used to be that basketball was my life. But now it's not. It's not as important as my child."

Sheryl couldn't stay away from basketball for long, however. A few days after she gave birth, she asked her doctor when she could return to the gym. The doctor told her that she could begin playing again whenever she wanted to, and two days later, Sheryl was working out. She lifted weights to regain her strength, ran laps, and shot basketballs over and over. After a few weeks, she could play in half-court games. About a month later, she started to play on a full court.

Sheryl still had her unique skills, but she was rusty. She also missed her son. "I'd be gone only two or three hours, and most of it was running to the phone. It was killing me to be away from my child." Sheryl's mother helped care for Jordan when Sheryl was at the gym, which made the new mother feel more

Coach Van Chancellor looks on as Sheryl shares the spotlight at a press conference with her new son, Jordan, who was named after her basketball super-star idol, Michael Jordan. Although delighted to be a mother, Sheryl missed playing and was anxious to get back in the game.

comfortable. By the end of July, she was confident enough to join the Houston Comets. As she told reporters, "Obviously I'm not in the shape I want to be in, but I feel I'm good enough to go back and help my team. . . . I don't expect to come in and score 25 to 30 points per game. But I think I'll be a good leader for the team and another offensive threat."

The Houston Comets had done well even without Sheryl, moving into second place in the WNBA's Eastern Conference. Their top player, Cynthia Cooper, had led the league in scoring, and Coach Chancellor had designed his team's offensive to fit Cooper's skills. He wasn't going to change his plans because Sheryl was now on the team.

After practicing with the Comets for a week, Sheryl played her first WNBA game on August 7, facing the Phoenix Mercury in Houston. The home crowd was excited that Sheryl was finally going to play, and the fans gave her a standing ovation. Sheryl also received roses from Charles Barkley, a star in the NBA. In the stands, baby Jordan slept peacefully with his father and grandmother.

Sheryl made her first appearance in the WNBA about 10 minutes into the game with Phoenix. The first time she touched the ball, she almost lost control of it. She only played for a few minutes and didn't take a shot, but she was happy with her performance. It felt good to be on the court. "I give myself an A plus," Sheryl said after the game. "I didn't have any turnovers or mistakes." She also admitted she was nervous. "It's going to take awhile to get the butterflies out."

Coach Chancellor was also pleased with Sheryl's performance. Still, he didn't want to use her much in the second half when the game was close. Knowing it would take time for Sheryl to be at her best, he commented, "Michael Jordan couldn't lay out a year, much less have a baby, and come back and be the same."

It took three more games for Sheryl to score her first points in the WNBA, against the

Utah Starzz. She scored midway through the first half, and a few minutes later, she hit two three-point shots in a row. The Comets went on to win 76-56. Sheryl finished with 18 points, six rebounds, and two assists. An excited Sheryl told reporters after the game, "I've been waiting for the moment, and tonight was my night. I'm just happy I scored more than two points."

Sheryl played five more games in the regular season, finishing with an average of 7.1 points per game. Her best game came on August 16 against the Charlotte Sting, when she scored 20 points. Houston finished the regular season with a record of 18 wins and 10 losses, the best in the league. The team would be in the playoffs, fighting to win the first WNBA championship.

For Sheryl, the playoffs were a tough period, and she spent most of her time sitting on the bench. In the semifinal game against the Charlotte Sting, Houston won 70-54, but Sheryl played only several minutes and didn't score a point.

In the title game of the playoffs, the Comets hosted the New York Liberty team. Both teams played strongly in the first half, although Houston held a slim lead. In the second half, the Comets began to steadily pull away from their rivals. Cynthia Cooper poured in 14 points, and the team played an excellent defense. Cooper finished with 25 points and led Houston to a 65-51 victory. Now Sheryl had a championship ring to go with her Olympic gold medal and NCAA championship. She had watched most of the game from the bench, however, and did not score.

Sheryl knew that having a baby had been

hard on her body and that she was not in the best shape. Still, she had impressed some observers by just trying to play. Val Ackerman, the chairman of the WNBA, commented that Sheryl "has broken new ground for women's basketball." When 1997 ended, Sheryl promised that the next year would be different. She told *People* magazine, "I want to show people, 'This is what you missed.'"

Sheryl gets past a Charlotte Sting guard and drives down the court. Returning to play in the WNBA, Sheryl needed several games to get her scoring up, but she still helped the Comets reach the WNBA playoffs.

6

PART OF
THE TEAM

S heryl got going on a very hectic schedule after the 1997 season ended. In October she became involved in a children's book club, which was set up on the Internet and encouraged kids to read. Already a children's book author, she had published *Bounce Back* in 1996—a book describing her life through the 1996 Summer Olympics.

The rising star also had the duties of being a mom. "That's a challenge in itself, a lot harder than playing basketball," she explained. Despite her responsibilities, however, Sheryl never stopped playing basketball while raising Jordan. She admitted that she had been over-weight after giving birth, and she knew she had to work hard to prepare for the next season. When 1998 rolled around, Sheryl was back to her usual 145 pounds.

Sheryl had been asked to play on the U.S. team competing at the World Championships that year, but she said no. The Comets began practice in late May and she wanted to spend all her energy working with her teammates. Some people wondered how Sheryl and Cynthia Cooper would get along. Cooper had been the hero of the 1997 championship

With teammates Tina Thompson (left) and Cynthia Cooper (right), Sheryl celebrates her return to the team and the Comets' 1998 championship. Her strength renewed, Sheryl played the season with everything she had, helping to lead the team to victory.

Guarding a Phoenix Mercury player, Sheryl shows how she became one of "The Big Three" in the WNBA. She had regained her quickness, improved the accuracy of her shots, and was fighting to regain her phenomenal scoring record.

and was named the WNBA's Most Valuable Player. Sheryl, however, was one of the league's best-known stars, and the WNBA featured her in many of its ads.

Cooper wasn't worried about her relationship with Sheryl. "I think it's going to work out," she said. "Sheryl is a great talent and we're working well together in practice. . . . We are both playing hard and intense. It makes for good practices." Sheryl commented that the Comets needed more than its two superstars to defend its league championship. She explained to reporters, "Honestly, it takes more than five players to win, I know that, Cynthia knows that."

The 1998 season began as the last one had ended—with Houston playing the New York Liberty. For Sheryl, this game was much more enjoyable than the previous one. Playing just 27 minutes, she scored 28 points, her career high in the WNBA. She was quick again and her shot was accurate. The old Sheryl Swoopes had returned to the court. Houston won the game and then added three more wins in a row. During those first four games, Sheryl averaged just under 20 points, 5.3 rebounds, and 2.5 steals per game.

In the third game, against the Cleveland Rockers, Sheryl scored 25 points, and her teammates Cynthia Cooper and Tina Thompson added another 44 points. These three players would soon be nicknamed "The Big Three," and their combined talent would make Houston hard to beat. With such scorers, Houston could count on winning even if one of the three had a bad game.

For Sheryl, her first bad game was just around the corner. On June 21, when the Comets faced the Los Angeles Sparks, Sheryl took 10 shots—and missed them all. She had one rebound, no steals, and no blocks. "I never, ever a day in my life played that bad," Sheryl said before her next game. "I just felt I was out there taking up space." In the following game against the Phoenix Mercury, however, she bounced back with 21 points. Unfortunately, her team didn't do as well, losing 69-66.

After that loss, Houston went on a roll, winning its next 11 games. Sheryl continued to play well, averaging almost 16 points a game. During that winning streak, however, she gave the Comets and their fans a scare. On July 2, while practicing with the team, she began to feel strange. Breaking into a sweat, she suddenly slumped to the floor.

Sheryl was rushed to the hospital where doctors performed a series of tests. Their conclusion: Sheryl was dehydrated (her body lacked fluids). She was given liquids and ordered to stay overnight. Her collapse had scared her and her teammates, and Sheryl knew she had to do something to prevent a recurrence.

Part of Sheryl's problem was that she was eating too much junk food. She could drink as many as six soft drinks a day instead of water, and she also liked sweets. After the fainting spell, doctors told Sheryl she had to improve her diet, and she promised to change her habits. "There's a Shipley's doughnut shop near my home that I have to pass each day on the way to practice," she said. "Now, when I pass, I have to turn my head and look the other way."

She missed the Comets' next game, but in a few days she was ready to play again. For the rest of the season, Sheryl and the Comets were almost unstoppable. They finished the regular season with 27 wins and just three defeats. Sheryl scored an average of 15.6 points per game, the sixth best in the league. She was also among the league's leaders in four other categories, including third in steals and three-pointers. Sheryl had her first double-double in the WNBA on June 30 and finished with four for the season. Along with Cynthia Cooper and Tina Thompson, Sheryl was named to the All-WNBA team, an honor showing her place as one of the best players in the league.

Ready to do her best in the season playoffs, Sheryl and the Comets first played the Charlotte Sting. This year, the two teams would play a best-of-three series, which means the first team to win two games would move on to the finals. The first game was in Charlotte, North Carolina, and it was a rough one. Cooper hurt her ankle and knee, Comet guard Kim Perrot played with a bad ankle, and during the game, Sheryl banged her left knee. The Comets were still too strong for the Sting, however, and they won 85-71. The team set a record for most points in a WNBA playoff game, with Cynthia Cooper scoring 27 points, while Sheryl added 17 points and eight rebounds.

Game two was played in Houston, and Sheryl had her first double-double in a playoff game, scoring 18 points and grabbing 13 rebounds—

her highest rebound total ever in the pros. After the game, Sheryl told reporters, "I kind of told myself that I wanted to work hard on the boards, offensively and defensively. And tonight I felt like I just happened to be at the right place at the right time." The Comets won 77-61. Again, they were going to the championships.

In the finals, the Comets faced the Phoenix Mercury, one of just three teams to beat them during the regular season. The top Phoenix players included Jennifer Gillom and Michelle Timms. Gillom had finished second to Cynthia Cooper in the voting for the league's MVP, and Timms was among the league leaders in assists. Once again, the Comets would play a best-of-three series, and once again, they were the visiting team for game one.

In that first game, Gillom was the star for the Mercury as the two teams battled back and forth. With less than a minute to go, the score was tied at 51. Perrot of the Comets tried to take a shot, but Gillom blocked it. At the other end of the court, Gillom scored with just nine seconds left. A Phoenix free throw in the last second put the score at 54-51. For the first time ever, Houston had lost a playoff game. Sheryl had not played her best, scoring just eight points. On the boards, though, she was once again out- standing, with 11 rebounds.

The Comets hoped their play would improve when they returned to Houston, but they trailed for much of game two. They were down by 12 with seven minutes and 24 seconds to play, when they began to come back. The Big Three all scored and helped give the Comets a one-point lead with two minutes to go. Phoenix tied the game with one minute left and then neither team could score. The game went into overtime.

The overtime period in the WNBA lasts five minutes. For almost two minutes, no one scored. Cooper finally got off a shot that found its way through the net, and Houston took the lead 68-66. After Phoenix made one free throw, Sheryl hit a 15-foot jump shot, and a basket by Gillom made the score 70-69 in Houston's favor. Then, with only one minute left, Sheryl hit another jump shot. "The only thing I saw was the basket," she said after the game. "I thought, 'This is my court. This is my game. I am not losing this game.' I always think my shot is going in, but this time I was sure of it." The Mercury did not score again. The final score was 74-69.

After the game, Sheryl talked about fighting back. "When we got down by about 10 points, the only people who believe[d] we could come back and win was our fans and us. We always believe[d] we could win this game." Sheryl also added a prediction for the third and final game: "We are going to win this thing Tuesday night."

As game three started, it seemed that Sheryl would be right. The Comets led throughout the first half, but early in the second half, the Mercury took the lead. The score remained close for several minutes, and with little more than seven minutes to play, Houston led by just one point. Then Sheryl began to show why she was one of the Big Three. She made two free throws to give Houston a 64-61 lead. A few seconds later, she made a great pass to Janeth Arcain, who scored. Another basket by Sheryl brought the score to 68-61.

The play of the game came a few minutes later. The score was 71-67 in Houston's favor, and Michelle Timms of the Mercury tried to get a shot off. On defense, Sheryl knocked over one of her own teammates as she leaped and

Holding her son and the Comets' 1998 WNBA victory trophy, Sheryl joins the team's victory parade in Houston. Following this triumph, Sheryl was sure she would be part of another championship team in 1999.

successfully blocked the ball. She later added two more free throws. Houston won 80-71, and the Comets were WNBA champions once again.

After the game, Coach Chancellor spoke with reporters, "Sheryl made some big-time free throws, shots, and rebounds. She's a big-time player." She finished with 16 points, six assists, and five rebounds and had proven what kind of professional player she really was. "I'm just really excited that I had the opportunity to come back and be a part of this wonderful organization," she said after the game. "I feel like I contributed a lot more this year than I did last year. . . . I look forward to doing it again."

7

THREE-PEAT

In January, before the 1999 WNBA season, Sheryl and other WNBA stars traveled to Europe and played against teams from Slovakia, France, and Hungary. With Sheryl's help, the U.S team won four out of five games.

When Sheryl returned to America, the Basketball Hall of Fame gave her a special honor. The Hall of Fame maintains an exhibit with models of the lockers of basketball stars, and for the first time the exhibit included the lockers of two women players—Sheryl and Rebecca Lobo.

The off-season was also a time of troubles for the Comets and for Sheryl. Teammate Kim Perrot announced she had cancer and would not be playing. Her struggle to fight the disease would affect Sheryl and her teammates all season. Sheryl also suffered a strain in her personal life when she filed for divorce from Eric. She found the divorce especially hard because Houston fans had gotten to know her family so well, but she assured her fans she would be ready to play. "I'm just trying to stay focused and do what I have to do on the court because this is my job," she promised.

What Sheryl and the Comets had to do was defend their

At the end of the 1999 season, Sheryl was delighted to pose with the Comets' three WNBA trophies won in three straight years. She could also be proud of her superb all-around play and high scores that helped lead her team to its championships.

championship. Few sports teams can dominate a league for so many years, and experts wondered if they could do that. For the Comets, their goal for the season was to earn a "three-peat"—that third straight championship.

The Comets started the season strong, winning their first seven games, some of which were spectacular games for Sheryl. In one game against the Utah Starzz, she scored 25 points, pulled down six rebounds, and made four steals. A few nights later in Los Angeles, she scored 25 again and added five rebounds, three steals, and three blocks.

Across the country, WNBA fans were noticing Sheryl's great season. For the first time, the WNBA was holding an All-Star game with the fans picking the starting players. The votes for Sheryl were pouring in. On July 6, the league announced that Sheryl had collected more votes than any other player and that she would be a starting forward for the Western Conference team. Joining her were the other two members of The Big Three—Cooper and Thompson.

Before the All-Star game, in answering fans' E-mail messages, Sheryl replied, "I never thought that I would be the top vote-getter in the first WNBA All-Star Game. However, I definitely consider it an honor and I'm very proud of that." The All-Star Game was held at New York City's Madison Square Garden. Sheryl played only 19 minutes but had eight points, eight rebounds and three steals. The Western Conference team won 79-61.

Back in the regular-season games with the Comets, Sheryl continued her high scoring and all-around dazzling play. When, on July 16, the Comets met the Utah Starzz, Houston at one point fell behind by 17. Sheryl came through and helped her team close the gap. She scored 11 of her team's next 13 points and tied the score. In overtime, Sheryl scored six points and Houston won 88-84. Sheryl finished the game with a career high of 33 points. In her next game, she led the Comets with 21 points, although they lost to the Los Angeles Sparks. For the week, Sheryl averaged an amazing 27 points, six rebounds, and five assists. The WNBA rewarded her performance by naming her Player of the Week. In a historic game against Detroit, her 14 points, 15 rebounds, and 10 assists gave her the first triple-double in WNBA history. Again, she was Player of the Week.

Sheryl holds an oversized All-Stars-game ballot. In the voting for starting players in the game, fans gave Sheryl more votes than any other player. It was a proud moment for Sheryl, who was determined to live up to the honor.

The season was going well for Sheryl and the Comets. The team was in first place, and she was again among the league leaders in many categories. Coach Chancellor commented about Sheryl, "She's improved all parts of her game. She's always been a great offensive player, but she's stepped up her defense and rebounding."

On August 19, the Comets received bad news: Kim Perrot had passed away. Despite receiving treatments, she could not defeat the cancer that had spread to her brain. The next day, tears flowed on the court as the Comets played the Sparks. Cooper, Perrot's best friend on the team, was too upset to play. The other Comets struggled through the game, losing 68-64. Although Sheryl led the Comets with 25 points, she was so saddened by the loss, that her game statistics meant very little to her.

Sheryl did not disappoint her many fans in the finals of the 1999 season. She attacked the basket and defended aggressively against the Los Angeles Sparks. Her playing was a significant factor in giving the Comets their final victory of the year.

The next game was the last of the regular season, and the Comets came back determined to win. In the first half, Sheryl collided with another player and sprained her knee. She left the game and did not return. With the playoffs about to start, Houston fans wondered if their star forward would be at her best. After the accident, Sheryl reported, "I thought I heard something pop, and it just really scared me, especially getting ready for the playoffs." She got some good news, however. The injury was not serious, and Sheryl could play. The Comets went on to win the game and finish with a season record of 26 wins and six losses, the best in the league.

In the first semifinal game, the Comets traveled to Los Angeles to play the Sparks. The Comets trailed at halftime by four, and in the second half, the Sparks played even better. With Lisa Leslie, the team's star player, scoring 23 points, the Sparks won 75-60. Sheryl led the Comets with 17 points, but she was not happy with her team's play. She commented, "I don't think we were aggressive offensively or defensively, like we've been all year."

The next game against the Sparks was played in Houston and a different Comet team showed up to play—one that could score and defend like champions. The Comets held the Sparks to just 55 points while scoring 83 points themselves. Sheryl, still bothered by her injured knee and an injured finger, scored only eight points but had six rebounds and two blocked shots.

In the final game of the series, both teams shot well at the start. Sheryl had a strong first half, scoring 16 points, and the game stayed close until Los Angeles scored 15 points while the Comets managed just two. The Sparks kept their lead for most of the second half, but the Comets fought back and pulled ahead. With the game almost over, Sheryl made a key play. She stole the ball and raced down the court for a layup that gave Houston an eight-point lead. The Comets went on to win 72-62, and Sheryl finished with 23 points and five steals. With the victory, the Comets were going to the WNBA finals for the third time. The hope for a three-peat lived on.

In the finals, Houston faced the New York Liberty once again. The Liberty had played the whole season without one of its top players, Rebecca Lobo. Other players, however, such as Teresa Weatherspoon, Vickie Johnson, and Crystal Robinson, had been outstanding. It seemed no surprise when, in the first game in New York, the Liberty took an early 3-2 lead. They never led again. Using tight defense, the Comets won 73-60. Cynthia Cooper had 29 points and Sheryl added 15 more.

Sheryl's biggest plays came on defense. She held Crystal Robinson, an excellent three–point shooter, to only 12 points. Coach Chancellor praised Sheryl's play. "She just denied the basketball all the time. . . . She was more physical tonight than she has been in three years for us defensively." After the game, Sheryl told reporters, "This was definitely a huge win for us. Hopefully we'll have the momentum going into game two with us."

The Liberty were not going to give up so easily, however. The series moved to Houston for game two. The Comets took an early lead, but New York fought back. With just seconds left, the score was tied at 65. Close to the basket, Tina Thompson shot—and scored. The Comets were ready to celebrate their third championship when, as the clock ran out, Liberty's Teresa Weatherspoon launched one last shot. From 50 feet away, she heaved the ball toward the basket. It bounced off the backboard and through the net. The Comets were stunned as New York won 68-67. A disbelieving Sheryl said, "Like everybody else probably thought, I didn't think it had any chance of going in."

The Comets had one last chance to earn their three-peat in the third and final game, and were relying on The Big Three. In the first half, Cynthia Cooper and Sheryl scored 20 of the team's first 22 points, and the Comets led at half time 33-25. Both teams played tight defense in the second half, and Cooper and Thompson carried the offense. The Comets held on to win 59-47. Cooper led all scorers with 24, while Sheryl had 11, and Thompson had 13. The Comets were champions for a third year in a row.

After the game, Sheryl told reporters that this was the best championship of the three. She also thought about the one Comet who wasn't part of the celebration—Kim Perrot. "Obviously," Sheryl said, "with Kim not being here, it was very emotional." Still, Sheryl and the Comets found some joy in their victory. "We are all happy and excited," Sheryl added. "The season didn't go the way we wanted it to, but it definitely ended the way we wanted."

What lay ahead for Sheryl Swoopes? She would like to play four or five more years and then perhaps try broadcasting. She also has her son to raise. For now, however, Sheryl has more time to show she's one of the greatest women basketball players of all time.

STATISTICS

COLLEGE

Year	Team	G	FGM	FGA	Pct.	FTM	FTA	Pct.	REB	AST	PTS	AVG
1989–90	South Plains	35	361	758	.476	141	191	.738	404	182	897	25.6
1990–91	South Plains	29	281	599	.469	123	179	.687	298	132	723	24.9
1991–92	Texas Tech	32	265	527	.503	135	167	.808	285	152	690	21.6
1992–93	Texas Tech	34	356	652	.546	211	243	.868	312	139	955	28.1
TOTALS		130	1263	2536	.498	610	780	.782	1299	605	3265	25.1

PROFESSIONAL

Year	Team	G	FGM	FGA	Pct.	FTM	FTA	Pct.	REB	AST	PTS	AVG
1997	Houston	9	25	53	.472	10	14	.714	15	7	64	7.1
1998	Houston	29	173	405	.427	71	86	.826	149	62	453	15.6
1999	Houston	32	226	489	.462	100	122	.820	202	127	585	18.3
TOTALS		70	424	947	.448	181	222	.815	366	196	1102	15.7

G	Games Played	FTA	Free Throws Attempted
FGM	Field Goals Made	REB	Rebounds
FGA	Field Goals Attempted	AST	Assists
Pct.	Percentage	PTS	Points
FTM	Free Throws Made	AVG	Average

CHRONOLOGY

1971	Born Sheryl Denise Swoopes on March 25 in Brownfield, Texas
1987	Named to the All-State team for girls' high school basketball in Texas
1988	Named to the All-State team for the second time; leads Brownfield to the state championship
1989	Makes All-State at Brownfield a third time; enrolls in the University of Texas but leaves school within a week; enrolls at South Plains Junior College
1991	Enrolls at Texas Tech; named an All-American and the Junior College Player of the Year
1993	Leads team to the national championship; named National Player of the Year; named Female Athlete of the Year; plays in Italy briefly; makes ad for Nike; joins the U.S. National Team, which tours and wins the World Championship
1995	Marries Eric Jackson
1996	Wins a gold medal with the U.S. women's basketball team at the Summer Olympics in Atlanta, Georgia
1997	Signs with WNBA; joins the Houston Comets; takes leave and gives birth to a son, Jordan Eric, on June 25; returns to Comets and plays only a few games in the WNBA's first season; Comets win the first WNBA championship
1998	Plays first full season with the Houston Comets; named to the All-WNBA team; Comets win the second WNBA championship
1999	Receives the most votes as starting player for the first WNBA All-Star game; achieves the first triple-double in the WNBA on July 27; helps the Comets win their third WNBA championship

FURTHER READING

Burby, Liza. *Sheryl Swoopes: All-Star Basketball Player.* New York: Rosen Publishing Group, 1998.

Knisley, Michael. "Swoopes's Dreams." *Sporting News*, May 22, 1995.

Sehnert, Chris. *Sheryl Swoopes.* Edina, MN: ADBO Publishing, 1998.

Swoopes, Sheryl. *Bounce Back.* Dallas: Taylor Publishing, 1996.

Welden, Amelie. *Girls Who Rocked the World: Heroines from Sacajawea to Sheryl.* Hillsboro, OR: Beyond Word Publishing, 1998.